I0706714

The Middle Urinal Experiment

Louie Springer

Pending Copyright © 2024 B.L. Springer

All rights reserved. No part of this publication may be reproduced, distributed, or transmitted in any form or by any means, including photocopying, recording, or other electronic or mechanical methods, without prior written permission of the publisher, with the exception of brief quotations embodied in critical reviews and certain other noncommercial uses permitted by copyright law. For permission requests, write to the author via e-mail at:
LouieSpringerStoryteller@gmail.com

Dedicated to the one who has always stood by my side no matter what, through my weirdness and wild ideas, through thick and thin…my beautiful wife.

And to my children- No matter how weird, wild, or crazy an idea might be, as long as if you go for it with good intentions, aim high and never give up. And if you don't succeed at first, then get up, dust yourself off, learn the lesson, and keep going.

Thank you to all who unintentionally were a part of the middle urinal experiment. Because of those who urinated in urinals next to me, this became possible.

That Tall Guy is Always Pissing at The Middle Urinal

You're out shopping at the home improvement store on a busy day, and that urge to pee sucker-punches your bladder. You hurry into the closest bathroom to find that only the middle urinal is open and notice both stalls are in use. Even though you have a sense of urgency at this very moment, the fact you have to urinate at the middle urinal stops you in your tracks to think about needing to use it. Even with these thoughts, you cannot hold it much longer, knowing you need to utilize the middle urinal no matter what. Your breathing becomes deep and heavy as your palms become sweaty, possibly due to how badly you must pee but primarily because you must use the middle urinal. Once you approach and settle in to conduct your business, the other men at the end urinals make a noise and slightly pivot their bodies away. Amid this, you're having performance issues due to being surrounded by everyone. You eventually produce a flow, giving you a slight sigh of relief. As you finish your business, you make sure not to make eye contact with anyone while attempting to get out of the bathroom, skipping the sinks, going back out into the world, away from the awkwardness of the public bathroom.

People commonly go to the bathroom multiple times a day, in various situations, at different times, with many outcomes. But talking about bathroom use has never been a thing. It's not exactly a topic of interest. However, one school paper would create a strange interest in making bathroom habits into a conversation piece.

Public bathrooms, in general, and middle urinals, specifically, bring out the best insecurities that many barely recognize they have. Most will deny that there are insecurities, even though no one knows how to talk about the bathroom beyond just saying, "I need to go to the bathroom." There is the common terminology we use while teaching children as pee and poop, which stick for a lifetime—or other terms, like answering nature's call, whizzing, and tinkling. Then, there is professional terminology, such as urine and bowel movements. Remember some masculine slang for urinating, like draining the vein or hosing out the toilet. And to women's credit, I don't know of any slang for women to urinate, maybe because there is less of a need to be macho. I've never heard a woman say, "Welp, I need to empty the old clam; she's getting full."

Beyond simply speaking about going to the bathroom, as there seem to be no good words for it, everyone must remember that urinating (and pooping) is part of the natural order as a living organism. It cannot be stopped; it has to happen, or we will become sick. And if it doesn't want to come out, no worries. We have tools to help with that as well.

However, where we get rid of our waste is more of a private matter and a more significant issue in society. At home, it's easy to maintain privacy (unless you have children), allowing you to be in that space alone to conduct your business and not have others looking at you. But once you leave your dwelling, it can be a challenge in public spaces, even more so if someone is bathroom shy and struggles with relieving themselves around others.

The creation of public bathrooms was to provide just enough privacy to conduct our excretion business in a quick and timely fashion. Many people are specific in maneuvering themselves in public bathrooms to provide extra space and privacy from other patrons. These actions and methods in public bathrooms have created unsaid rules of how people should operate while relieving themselves in these types of spaces. But these unsaid rules are rarely spoken of or taught explicitly to us. We as humans learn through our experiences of using public bathrooms and observing how others act. Ironically, these unsaid rules have become a common standard by many while in public bathrooms, which in current day can be noted by the various content on social media discussing public bathroom use.

But what if someone does not follow the unsaid public bathroom rules? How would others act and respond?

The middle urinal experiment broke most public bathroom rules, at least in the men's public bathroom, primarily focusing on the urinals. It was supposed to only be a community college sociology course paper as I tried to navigate my way through school as an adult learner. But it allowed for something discreetly documented in the past to be put down in poorly formed hard data based on raw observations in public bathrooms, as I specifically broke unsaid rules by urinating in the middle urinal no matter what. Granted, I may not have been the best candidate to piss strictly in the middle urinal standing at six foot and six inches tall with sleeve tattoos. But it's ok; we all survived.

Over time, I recognized that there was something more to the middle urinal experiment beyond a paper written in community college. To this day, conversations transpire about public bathroom use, specifically the middle urinal, and how men avoid it. It's an embarrassing and intriguing subject to many. The middle urinal experiment allowed me to focus and understand these elements at a depth most people usually could care less about.

The best part is that the experiment has not gone unforgotten. I've had people who knew of it bring it up in front of others who did not, sparking a conversation and making me realize that people want to talk about public bathroom use. Still, usually, we never do, most likely due to its social awkwardness.

Things tend to get weird after a few drinks with people who get excited about me going to the bathroom, sometimes asking, "Hey man, you going to piss in the middle urinal?" with a smirk on their faces as if I was about to be some rouge pisser breaking all the rules. They usually make the situation even more awkward as they attempt to watch others we don't know and giggle while I'm standing at the middle urinal. While alone these days, I don't always choose to go to the middle urinal each time anymore, but there are plenty of times I feel compelled to do so as a good reminder of the time I strictly used the middle urinal and how uncomfortable it makes others.

As much fun it is to talk about the middle urinal experiment and public bathroom use, it displays the concept of social awkwardness during necessary times. We must do it, so we do it, even if we are weird about it—the idea of just doing your business and then getting out. Or at least that's the idea.

Social awkwardness in America is an ever-changing beast. We often find ways to make socially awkward concepts seem normal while making what should be standard concepts appear as socially awkward if it does not align with current societal beliefs. I recognize reading that sounds odd, but read that last sentence again.

Social awkwardness is not unknown; we just have turned our cheeks the other way. There is a variety of topics that have social awkwardness embedded in them. Examples include cell phones, food systems, sexuality topics, and medicinal beliefs. These topics could be considered complex social awkwardness. But there is also what I consider simple social awkwardness. This awkwardness is when we learn to live life with specific tools and don't understand the world when we do not have them.

I will use the "microwave conundrum" to explain this idea.

When my wife and I bought our house, it had no microwave. It also had no dishwasher. People did not find it awkward that we did not have a dishwasher; they were just frustrated for us. However, with no microwave present in the house, people lost their crap. We decided not to buy one for a while, trying to live without it. And for the most part, we did just fine without a microwave.

Our friends and family became awkward about heating things without a microwave. They were unsure of themselves. It did not matter that we had not just one but two stoves. People would be slightly stressed, questioning how to warm or heat something quickly. We would then pull out a pot or pan and heat it on the stove. It just took a few extra minutes. It was not uncommon to have others react with a light laugh at how unbelievable and savage we were living because we did not have a microwave. Of all the things, this made us socially awkward to others since we did not have this standard household tool.

No worries, we now have a microwave. And a dishwasher. Also, you should try warming up a slice of pizza on a frying pan sometime. You will be happy you did.

The middle urinal experiment is a simple, socially awkward concept due to the nature of the task, which is essential and straightforward. However, it also expands into unsaid rules and expectations of our society, making it complex. These unsaid rules can be challenging to identify but are present in key situations, like public bathrooms. The recent pandemic also created some of these rules and expectations by the thought of becoming ill and how to avoid that possibility drastically.

An intriguing aspect of the middle urinal experiment is that most of the ideas and observations noted have stayed the same over the years since I conducted the experiment. Similar actions happen when I use the middle urinal now, as they did almost a decade ago when I wrote the college paper. However, I've also noticed an uptick in private bathrooms and more giant walls between urinals in establishments since the initial time frame of the experiment. These barriers have helped eliminate some unwanted awkward moments in public bathrooms.

But who am I to make these observations and write about public bathroom use and social awkwardness?

The answer is just a very observant guy. I am a self-proclaimed sociologist (I have no formal education to consider myself one academically) who wants to share noted observations for the betterment of our communities. To make others aware in their everyday life and break some of the standards created by our societal rules that should be disregarded. Like pissing in the middle urinal and toxic masculinity.

I have not always been outgoing and willing to test the waters of social rules. I grew up shy and reclusive, not entirely by choice. I would get around other people and shut down. I never really knew what to say or how to act (sometimes, I still don't). Occasionally, I would be challenged to do things that would put me in the spotlight. And depending on the moment, I either backed down into my corner or I would play along to a point that was safe for me. I never went full throttle.

Until I hit a point where I found some form of confidence and decided to be free, I began taking on life and awkward situations with no shame or concern, learning the ropes of society to become a functioning member. But previously, being a shy kid, I wanted to push my limits to discover what I could do. So, I began streaking as a consistent hobby and party trick. And it wasn't uncommon of others wanting to join in.

At eighteen, I pushed my limits to one of my most considerable extremes.

After a summer of traveling Europe and experiencing various cultures, I attended community college (the same one I would later in life conduct the middle urinal experiment). While in Europe, I discovered many art museums, and one thing that was common in the paintings and other art was the naked human body. The figures posed in various ways or were doing some task in their birthday suits. The artists appreciated the nude body and the presence it brought to their art. But of course, this type of art became less valued or shared in our current culture as the years passed.

During my first semester of college, my friends and I came across an ad on the wall that was looking for willing participants to pose nude in art classes. My buddies chuckled…I took down the information and followed up.

In no time, I became a nude model for art classes.

I remember the first time posing, not being sure what to expect. I walked out in front of a relatively large class with my robe on, stepped onto the small stage, dropped the robe, and moved my body into random positions for extended periods. The room was cold, my nipples were hard, and things shrunk. I did not look at anyone's face while nude. Instead, I stared at the fire alarm on the wall, laughing at what I had gotten myself into.

As I continued to pose naked often for different classes, I became comfortable in this environment and those around me in it. I looked at the students in the room more and interacted more with them during breaks. I did not recognize it then, but later, I realized the pillar of confidence this would build within' my soul.

The exciting and socially awkward part was that I had some classes with a few of the art students. It was a mutually agreed moment of them being in that art class and me posing nude. Still, once confronted in other classes with having to be in groups with me or create simple conversations, it became a roadblock for them due to me being the naked guy from their art class. There were some outlier individuals, but even some of them would mention to me how "brave" I was to be able to sit in front of a class naked like that because they wouldn't be able to do it.

I never felt odd while around these people. I posed for several different art classes, and there was a good amount of people who had seen me naked that I would see around the college. I would laugh and be intrigued by how people would be disengaged with me or struggle to find words.

This blip of time would last for two semesters of my life. The experience would encourage me to continue to do things in a way that was not common or did not walk the beaten path of society. I enjoyed noting other individuals' reactions to something that did not align with societal rules. However, I was young and just having fun. I did not fully consider what I was doing, but these times helped create the social observer I am today.

The military was the next piece that built me up with confidence and the ability to perform under pressure in various situations, including while at the middle urinal. As with many people, college did not pan out for me. I dropped out and ended up joining the United States Army. I had many experiences and times in the Army, but the most important that would help in the middle urinal experiment was the breaking of privacy.

Privacy was eliminated right from the beginning of basic training. Stripped down to just your underwear, standing in line with other people waiting for uniforms, but before you do, have a quick medical examination in an open corner where others can see you. And let's not forget about being lined up staring at a wall pulling out a butt cheek to get an injection. That was just the first day.

For the bathroom, everyone lined up, went to the first urinal available (and there were no portioned walls between each urinal), pooped at the first open stall (without a door), and used open showers with no space between one another. There was no choice or leisure; you just did it. And you did this to become comfortable with the idea that it did not matter if someone was already at a urinal or stall. You were to complete your bathroom business effectively and get out without lolly-gagging.

The bathroom in the barracks at my first unit was a large public bathroom. It had a little more privacy, but the walls and curtains did not mean much to us; it was just there. The areas designated as bathrooms overseas varied depending on the situation. Sometimes, we had to build our toilets to burn off our human waste with fuel. I can think of a time or two while I was attempting to have a good poop, and the individual on crap station duty moved the half barrel beneath my ass out from under me. I would yell out, "Hey man, I'm trying to shit," and the person on bathroom duty would quickly slide a new half barrel under me, saying, "Sorry bro, just trying to get this done." And I rightfully understood as I had been on that duty plenty of times.

These small moments helped build me up to become an open individual in the public to many things, allowing me to eventually be willing enough to create and conduct the middle urinal experiment.

Since those days, I've had moments of being extra and willing to put myself in awkward situations, especially in public bathrooms. It's a topic that I'm sure will always be relished on. And with that said, enjoy the middle urinal experiment and live life wild at the most random times in the weirdest ways!

The Whizzing Idea

It was the beginning of a cold spring semester in upstate New York. The winter had beaten us down, but as always, life continued. My schedule was all over the place, with a sociology class two times a week in the evening. The class was primarily adult learners attempting to create a new or better path in life, with a younger professor who seemed eager to teach. It could have been the start of a bland, typical semester to get another prerequisite out of the way.

However, the professor kept the conversations exciting and engaged us to be social observers, making the class fun. We covered the curriculum topics but also discussed odd bits and pieces—current events, previous careers, personal experiences, and how sociology played a role. I latched onto these conversations as someone who appreciated and observed various cultures, religions, and people.

As is the case in most college classes, we had papers and projects. Within' those papers and projects, a primary paper involved doing specific social observations in our communities around us to record data and then write about what was distinguished. It was going to take up extra time beyond the class.

Many people, including myself, grumbled about this as time was limited. With that thought in mind, people were coming up with ideas to do on the college campus. They figured it wouldn't involve much traveling, could be done randomly between classes, and was straightforward. I did not blame them one bit. It was not as if these projects and papers would make us famous sociologists.

Collectively, as a class, we shared plenty of ideas and thoughts, including observing cell phone usage in various places, observing individuals at a sandwich shop at specific hours, observing types of clothing people choose to wear who were in certain kinds of classes, and other random ideas. We had a melting pot full of discussion and thought.

Amid these conversations, I had to pee. No big deal, right?

I went to the men's room, and at that moment of all times, when the college was not as busy, only the middle urinal was open. I laughed, thinking, "Of course it is," and bravely went to the middle

urinal to do my business. I noticed that the one guy to my left didn't

budge, but for some reason, I looked at his face, and I think he

noticed. He was staring upward at the wall towards the ceiling,

trying to mind his own business. I then recognized that the guy to my

right slightly pivoted away from me. I started laughing out loud

about what I noticed while recognizing my thoughts when I first

walked in with only the middle urinal available. My laughing made

the two guys I was in between more uncomfortable as I looked over

and saw their faces turning red, and they attempted to hustle out of

the bathroom.

This acknowledgment of my reaction and the actions of the

others at the urinals ignited a fire in my brain...with maybe a few

dribbles on my shoes, to eagerly tell the class of my idea.

The conversation in the classroom seemed like it was

wrapping up, but I decided to blurt out, "So I just came up with an

idea." I explained what had just occurred when I went to the

bathroom, and it sparked both laughter and conversation. The other

men in the class hilariously agreed that the middle urinal is a last resort use in most cases unless it's someone you know, but even then, they still space out if they can. Through this conversation, the males in the class agreed that there was an unsaid rule of not using the middle urinal if other urinals or if a stall were available.

This conversation created a path to other topics about public bathrooms to think about. We began to question if this behavior of the middle urinal occurred when men were boys and, if not, when we, as males, learned these behaviors. We talked about locker rooms and other places where people are less ashamed of themselves than public bathrooms. Women's behavior in public bathrooms also became a conversation piece. There were some rules or habits standard as well that were unsaid in the women's bathroom per the individuals in the class.

The crucial factor of this conversation was that it was acknowledged and agreed by all that there were these unwritten and unsaid rules of public bathrooms for both men and women, especially with the urinals. Expectations that were never formally established instead were learned behaviors from observing, accepting, and adopting the actions of the community we grew up in.

Before we knew it, the class only had ten more minutes, and we had spent nearly an hour discussing public bathroom use, which I established as the topic for my observation paper. The class was dismissed early that evening, but the professor asked me to stay back for a few minutes. She gave me a simple warning for my observation choice during this short time.

"It's a great idea, but you need to know that you will also be pushing the boundaries of people's bubbles at a time when they are not expecting them to be. You will need to be mindful of how people will react and be able to back down if they become upset or abrupt," the professor stated, showing slight concern over my choice of what was supposed to be a simple college paper. But I understood her warning and gave my guarantee I would not try to overdo it.

Before officially starting the middle urinal experiment, I had to create a simple thesis and layout of how to track my results. I knew I needed to make sure that anyone who ended up being an unknown participant could not be identified in any way. I needed different elements to conduct while at the middle urinal, as in conversation or whistling, to collect data on some extremes. I also had to figure out how to interview people about bathroom habits

without being overly creepy.

I had my work cut out for me.

Piss Poor Planning Achieves Piss Poor Results

The planning phase for the middle urinal experiment became consistent for me. Not only was I planning on the way I would collect data, or even better, what data I would collect, but I also needed to build my confidence during this time. So I began urinating at the middle urinal at all times without observing others for the experiment, but rather to ensure I was over any personal mindset hurdles to its use. I worked diligently during the planning phase to figure out how I would physically and academically approach all aspects of the middle urinal. I had no time to waste as the semester seemed long, but it was not, especially if I wanted to collect solid data and have time to write a top-notch community college sociology paper.

Since this type of experiment had limited data from a lack of previous similar experiments, I had to create specific vital phrases and objectives. I decided to use makeshift terminology of the urinal buffer rule, meaning that there is an unsaid rule that you don't use the urinal next to the other man unless if its absolute dire straits. I

identified the characteristics of simple reactions, such as looking

away or a minor pivot towards the opposite direction, compared to

major responses, like a significant pivot away or making sighing

noises to even vocalizing distraught. It seemed farfetched, but I

would learn that it was not.

I had to make decisions on the location of these observations

as well. Was I only going to use one or two specific public

bathrooms, or should I use all public bathrooms? The goal was to

stick to bathrooms primarily with three urinals, a general standard in

many men's public bathrooms, as if they created them with the urinal

buffer rule in mind. I decided that if I observed all public bathrooms,

as long as they met the three urinal conditions, I could collect data

on various groups to find common trends. I could then establish

findings on a broader range, not confined to one or two locations that

harbor the same groups of people.

When deciphering data collection, I first decided to note the

environment in each observation. I intended to register if it was a

typical bathroom setup or if there was anything special about the layout. I also wanted to track if I was the only one in the bathroom or if there were other urinating participants at either urinal on each side upon my arrival.

I thought about what if all the urinals were in use and the middle one didn't become available first. I decided that if I waited specifically for the middle urinal, that would make me creepier than I already intended. Those instances would become void from the data collection.

Next, I needed to note any immediate reactions that would occur on my initial approach to the middle urinal. The inspiration for me to get to this moment was how the other two men at the urinals on each side of me reacted—looking up and away, angling away from me as I approached the middle urinal. It was their way of acknowledging that someone was using the middle urinal, a significant element I wanted to capture in the experiment.

There needed to be an option to enhance the observation at my discretion while using the middle urinal. Being a public bathroom where people share a common interest in eliminating human waste, why couldn't some conversation be involved? Topics of common interest, nothing wild. Something like, "The weather is pretty rough today." Or if someone was wearing a sports team shirt, "That was a good game last night." Prominent topics, not anything like telling the man standing at the urinal next to me that he is wearing a nice watch.

Once I finalized the data to be collected, I created a tracking sheet. For obvious reasons, I did not bring the sheet into the bathroom or walk right out and input the data. I decided this would be conflicting for people coming and going from the bathroom and possibly create unintentional reactions due to my awkwardness in holding a piece of paper and marking items down. Instead, I took mental notes and would fill them out later in a less conflicting area.

I had all my plans and an idea of how to approach this experiment. However, as a man of science (so I claim), I still needed one key piece of the experiment—a thesis. I needed to make clear my objective and purpose for the middle urinal experiment.

Yes, I was looking for reactions and ultimately making people feel uncomfortable by doing something that should be acceptable. But I needed to go deeper with the idea. It needed to be more than just reactions. It needed to observe social awkwardness, human behaviors, and an unsaid understanding of proper public bathroom etiquette. I knew whatever I came up with would not be a standard or clean thesis but rather follow suit in how abnormal this experiment would become.

The thesis created for the middle urinal experiment ended up being, "Even though there is a middle urinal for use in most men's public bathrooms, many patrons follow unsaid rules that the middle urinal is not to be used unless the last option, creating uneasy tension when a patron uses the middle urinal at unnecessary times."

As I said, it was not a clean thesis, but there was nothing clean overall about this social experiment.

Chamber Pots, Water Closets, and Urinal Cakes:

A Brief History of Public Bathrooms

When thinking about it, the times when plumbing was barely a thing and the idea of public bathrooms, or even modern bathrooms in homes, really are not too far in the past. In smaller, rural towns, you might see an old outhouse sitting away from a house in someone's yard or find the ancient remnants of where one once stood.

The thought of using an outhouse is appalling to some. But we created that thought because of our modernization of plumbing and sanitary techniques. Obviously, this modernization is not bad because I would much rather hang out in my underwear in my heated house on a cold day and have my morning constitution rather than putting on cold weather gear to hike to the outhouse. But it is interesting to note the social behaviors created with the advancement of plumbing and ridding of our bodily waste.

Throughout history, the chosen spot for someone to eliminate waste has always been a unique topic. We, humans, have always known that we needed to get rid of our urine and bowel movements in some organized form or fashion and that we could not just excrete our nuggets and juice on the floor. But until the last century and a half-ish, there were struggles in disposing of human waste appropriately or a lack of knowledge about the harms it could have. The tree line used to be a common potty option in rural areas, but in larger built-up communities, people would use chamber pots and other forms of collecting waste and then empty them elsewhere.

As advancements in everyday life occurred, so did ideas for human waste removal. Proper human waste removal was necessary because some intelligent people recognized that improper sanitation methods affected the health of overall communities. The area where people went to the bathroom could affect drinking water and the soil food was grown in, causing other diseases and issues when consumed. Common diseases with poor sanitation include cholera, dysentery, hepatitis A, typhoid, polio, gastroenteritis, giardiasis, Escherichia coli (long name for e. coli), leptospirosis, and other fun little diseases and microbial bacterial illnesses. Unlike now, where we can test and figure out these diseases to treat reasonably quickly, they couldn't back then, often causing increased medical needs that could not be achieved, which would cause death. Dehydration is a common symptom in the noted illnesses, which in today's world is often very easy to treat, but in the history books, it was an effective killer.

We had to learn from our ancestors and those who inhabited the world's lands by their ill fates to figure out sanitation measures and best practices, which came with trial and error. This included recognizing the distance from a drinking source or garden compared to a human waste area, plus the geography of the land for the where and how deep to dig a human waste hole. As society increased its knowledge of proper human waste disposal, the health of communities improved.

Per the National Museum of American History, in the 1880s, the "germ theory" was increasing throughout the United States, noting the previously mentioned issues. Potty brainstorming individuals had to come together to work on longer-term, sustainable solutions.

In the 1890s, adequate toilets slowly became a thing in the water closet (water closets were basic bathrooms). Toilets were wash-down siphon bowl models that held five to seven gallons of water in a tank much higher than the toilet, which needed to be filled with buckets of water to use (there were no active water pumps yet as we have in today's world). After an individual was through with their business, they pulled a cord and water from that tank rushed into the toilet, and pushed the waste out. Along with this advancement came new ideas of how to have waste effectively be moved from the point of human excretion to a place where it could be held and processed. This idea was a science project that I will not get into, but with time, this became a healthy sanitation and sewer system for the disposing of human waste.

It's also important to note that toilet paper was created during this time. Before toilets and sewage systems, people often wiped their cracks and holes with corncobs, old newspapers, and other items considered easy to use. However, people recognized that these items, especially corncobs, jammed toilets and sewer systems. With that, one of these potty brains created toilet paper, which has advanced into what we have today to keep our soiled holes clean and not torn up.

It's important to discuss how there was no separation between males and females regarding the areas used. Everyone urinated and popped a squat in the same space with little privacy. The water closet increased privacy for conducting business; however, everyone shared the space. The issue with this is simple…men and women have different cleanliness needs while ridding of waste.

In the early 1900s, public groups advocated the creation of public water closets for use as needed, becoming known as comfort stations and restrooms. Continued concerns about inadequate privacy, safety, and cleanliness remained a conversation, especially for women, discouraging the use of these water closets.

During this time, people started thinking more about how humans have two different types of genitalia and how each disposes of urine and other bodily functions with additional needs. With this thought process, businesses and other public areas slowly began creating separate men's and women's restrooms. Laws slowly came into existence to help maintain order with the separate bathrooms. The continuous evolution of male and female public bathrooms has led us to our current day, where most establishments provide these separated areas.

The history of urinals is unique and varied in this timeline of public bathrooms.

Different types of urinals can be found throughout history, showing that critical civilizations and peoples recognized the need for a place for men (and possibly women, too, depending on their rules) to urinate. There have been discoveries of clay pots dug into the ground with stones on either side to indicate where to place your feet for good aim while peeing. There are records acknowledging that there were different types of tubes dug into the ground for men to urinate into. However, since there was not any running water, a build-up of urine seemed to be an issue as it overly saturated the ground around these pissing points. And, of course, one can assume that privacy in these areas was also limited.

That is until a man named Andrew Rankin in the 1860s created a patent for what he called rightfully a urinal bowl. With his patent, he wanted to develop a system that would receive urine and get rid of it into a sewer-type system to help with the "obnoxious and unpleasant odors emitted from urine discharge" but also make for increased privacy for each individual using the urinal. His initial ideas began with a giant trough-type urinal with minor partitions, allowing multiple men to urinate at the same time while not exposing their genitals to one another. But nowhere in the patent did it discuss a buffer rule between each spot and where each pissing participant should stand.

Rankin's urinal bowl idea would slowly gain traction, and everyone wanted to piss in one. Larger communities like cities had to increase their water supply significantly to support a proper sewer system with the amount of urine going into them. It took time for the system to be fully figured out and become effective, which was still very simple compared to the sewer systems in municipals today.

During the Industrial Revolution in the United States, urinals made a massive boom as factory owners recognized that urinals were quick and convenient for men to use and then return to work compared to other bathroom choices. This idea of multiple urinals in the workplace for employees picked up steam and became a thing. It assisted with decreasing wait time and increasing factory productivity. Many workplaces with working lines for productivity continue to follow this idea, having at least two urinals, if not many more, in the men's bathroom.

Beyond workplace establishments, it would be odd to find a single urinal in any establishment unless the bathroom is private, which has increased in popularity in recent years with individual unisex bathrooms. The three-urinal setup is in many places today, but now, what establishments are putting in place is a lower urinal for vertically challenged people and children as part of the setup. I'm waiting for the day they place higher-up urinals so that taller people don't splash their pee as much due to the force it hits the porcelain from their height.

The history of how we as a community use public bathrooms is rare knowledge. Back when I was conducting the experiment, I found some opinionated professional theories that discuss how we have slowly become prude as a society, causing the urge to want more privacy in public bathrooms and how there are fears of encountering others in public bathrooms and people in societies have created habits that are followed to achieve increased privacy. In more recent times, there are many funny social media discussions, memes, and videos about public bathrooms and how to use them, especially with urinals and the buffer rule. Still, there is no factual history of this information. It's always been a hush-hush topic because, seriously, who wants to talk about using the bathroom?

Ultimately, the history of public bathrooms and urinals is rich in its own right, but how we have used them, especially as we expanded into the public bathrooms we use today, has been challenging to follow. Over time, specific standard societal rules were created and influenced, and people followed them without understanding how it happened, as there was no open discussion on these topics. Interestingly, most people will say, "I never heard of such a thing," but when you ask about their public bathroom use, their routine often goes hand in hand with the standard societal rules of public bathrooms.

And how do I know that? Well, I asked people, of course, convincing others to talk to me about their bathroom habits.

Yo Buddy, Do You Piss in the Middle Urinal Ever?

Even though there had been plenty of discussion in the class when I thought of the idea, I wanted to get more information directly from other random men about their public bathroom use. Gain insight from their process and how they operate in a public bathroom.

My attempt at this was vague due to recognizing that I could end up at a middle urinal soon with any men participating in the discussions. How weird would that be? First, I asked about their public bathroom habits, and then I was at the middle urinal, possibly trying to have a simple conversation with them. Instead, I was fortunate to have made a few friends at college who hung around different groups of people. I would act like I was talking to this individual and then interject myself into the group conversation. Occasionally, in a study nook where it would be quiet if someone became talkative with me, I would pose the question loudly for everyone to hear besides the person talking to me.

"Hey, here's a random question for the men of the group: When you go into the bathroom here at school or any public bathroom, do you use the middle urinal?" I would use this line or one similar to spark the conversation. Many times, it would produce immediate silence with hints of light laughter. I could tell people were shocked or embarrassed that I would even ask about the bathroom, as if adults shouldn't discuss their toileting routines. That is why laughter happened when I posed the question. When we are nervous, uncertain, or odd about a situation, human nature often tends to "giggle". To ease the initial feelings of this moment, I would crack a few jokes while mentioning the sociology class and how I was attempting to work on a project about public bathrooms. Usually, this would calm people down, allowing them to open up to my questioning about public bathrooms.

The goal was to discuss in a group because I was using the idea to get one person talking to get everyone talking. This idea often worked. I could facilitate an offhand conversation with other men (and eventually women) as long as one person besides myself would open up. Sometimes, it would be that friend in the group I stopped to talk to that would help with this idea, other times it would be the alpha-looking individual of the group showing no fear to answer my question.

Once I started obtaining answers to my question, most men stated that they avoided the middle urinal in everyday, typical life. Of course, a few gentlemen said they would use it with no problem if it were the only option upon arriving in the bathroom. Or if in a busy public place, as in sporting events, concerts, or other large public events, there was no thought process to it; the first urinal, no matter where, was to be used to get in and out. A common answer was that if the two end urinals were already in use and only the middle urinal was open, many men said they would quickly see if a stall was available. If so, they would use that before using the middle urinal.

Opening my conversations with a single question about bathroom use, I quickly established that middle urinal avoidance was a thing, so I would try to figure out where men learned these ideas and behaviors. I often referenced my childhood and the lack of rules as an elementary school child. Everyone would pee wherever and have stupid urinating competitions in the bathroom. But then, at some point, the bathroom rules started coming into play.

Again, many agreed and acknowledged that it was also like this for them. They were unsure where they learned the rules, but it started occurring like an instinct. I began deciphering that most, if not all, of the men who participated in the conversations noted it was a learned human pattern and behavior of the public bathroom through experiences and personal interactions.

Of course, some individuals were outliers who gave specific reasons for not using the middle urinal. I had one or two people say that vital male figures in their childhood would make mean or disturbing comments about people who use the middle urinal in public bathrooms. I will let you use your imagination for those comments shared with me. Other outliers had a bad experience in the past while using the middle urinal that influenced their beliefs. One of these outliers shared a story of a time in high school.

As most of society legally should know, we do not consider someone an adult until they are 18. Graduating from high school is a type of passage into adulthood. Usually, when boys reach high school, they know to follow the middle urinal rules. How they react to others using the middle urinal and their attitudes is a reflection of the environment they had been raised in.

This outlier explained that he had to urinate so badly during an event when he was a junior in high school that the only urinal open was the middle one. When he went to the urinal to relieve himself, he said one of the other students beside him started making rude comments about him using the middle urinal. Others then began to make comments as well. When he finished urinating, he went to wash his hands with one of the other bathroom patrons asking sarcastically, "You going to use the middle sink too…" and I will not finish the statement. These asshole individuals continued to make comments about this moment in time, even beyond the bathroom. This occurrence might not sound like much but it was enough to mentally affect this individual to the point that they firmly claimed they would never use the middle urinal again and was very cautious while in public bathrooms.

Overall, it was established through the conversations that there are rules in public bathrooms for men, with the biggest evolved around the middle urinal. However, most men were unsure of how the unsaid rules of the middle urinal and public bathrooms were established for them to follow. Instead, it seemed as if societal actions in public bathrooms created these rules unintentionally, and the majority began following along as they aged to the point of understanding. Unfortunately, as noted with the outlier discussed, some people experience negative moments in public bathrooms that cause harm to an individual mentally, providing them with more of a hard reason as to why they have severe avoidance while in public bathrooms. But ultimately, in everyday life, the idea of proper use of public bathrooms by men is silently agreed upon and followed by all.

With these conversations in mind, it was now time for me to take action and find my way to all the middle urinals!

The Middle Pisser

I felt prepared for the middle urinal experiment once I figured everything out. I had already urinated primarily in the middle urinal for a week or two prior, building up my confidence without doing an official observation. I had all the planning I needed to collect data. It was now time to initiate and execute the experiment in total capacity.

I scoped out all the college bathrooms in preparation to know their setup, locations, and what class I would be in during that part of the day to assist me in being ready for my data collection. I also checked out other public bathrooms in places I frequented, including grocery stores, home improvement stores, and several other establishments. It was difficult to mark the observations beyond the college, but I would make a note on my cell phone with a text to my email.

The first observation took place at one of the busiest bathrooms on campus. It was in a central hallway, near at least two primary entrances to the campus, with plenty of passersby. The unique thing about this bathroom was a random stall wall placed by the urinals. There was a direct view of the urinals from the hallway if the wall had not been present. Also, it was a handicapped bathroom, so it had an automatic button that would leave the door open for an extended time. I found this funny. Others did not and may have been having performance issues before the placement of this wall.

The great thing about this wall for the experiment was that it made the space slightly tighter and awkward, which I annotated in my data collection. This wall would make other bathroom patrons have issues effectively escaping the area from me using the middle urinal without it becoming weird, especially if people were wearing backpacks. I did not want to trap people, but over time, observations in this bathroom would become some of the most interesting because of the obstacle everyone had to get around to use the urinals.

During this observation, someone was already at the left urinal, and the other two were open. When I went to the middle urinal instead of the other end, I could tell from the corner of my eye that this other man urinating kept looking at me oddly but also slightly pivoted in the other direction. When he finished, I could hear him slide what I'm assuming was his arm against the wall that blocked the urinals from the door to stay as far away from me as he could. As he went out, a new person who used the other end of the urinals came in.

I decided to say to this person, "Crappy day to drive into school, huh?" and they attempted to respond while looking down towards the urinal. But his response was, "Mmm, uhhh, yeah…uhhhh, yep." That was about as much as I would get out of him. I then finished up, washed my hands, and went on my way. Nothing weird or crazy.

Many observations from this point on would go like this. The slight pivot to the other direction, away from me, was the most common move other urinators would make. If not a pivot, some men would attempt to "hug" the urinal, meaning they would step forward or lean inward towards it to get their body as close as possible to the urinal. It did not matter if I started with others already present in the bathroom or alone, and people approached the urinals. Most other men would automatically conduct one of these actions noted, some more noticeable than others. It's challenging to go from standing still to pee to slightly moving your body to hide from the guy at the middle urinal without anyone noticing.

Some patrons in the bathroom would pivot too much, which would be noticed by a slight splashing sound on the floor. They would then scramble to correct their aim back into the urinal. When this would happen, it was not uncommon to note increased reactions from these individuals by either heavy sighing or saying things under their breath. But I knew they were screaming inside their heads and possibly imagining slamming my head into the wall.

Another common reaction noted was the avoiders. These individuals would come into the bathroom needing to urinate but immediately see that the urinal buffer rule had been broken. They did not want to put themselves in the situation of having to urinate next to another man. If there were a stall open, they would immediately go that route. If not, I noticed people would go over to the sink and act as if they were checking out an ingrown hair on their face. They would move over to the urinals once I had moved on from the middle urinal. Some people would ultimately leave the bathroom. If I were lucky enough, I would see someone in the hallway near the bathroom, keeping watch of the door as I exited. As I walked out, they would go in. I assumed in those situations that they were the person who fled the bathroom after seeing the middle urinal buffer broken.

The noises made during these observations were also an impressive finding. It would be quiet in the bathroom, with just the slight trickle sound of urine hitting porcelain until I would stand at the middle urinal. It was not uncommon for people to make a low grumble or act like they were clearing their throats. Many men did this weird blowing air out of their mouths thing where it sounded like maybe they were in pain or holding their breath while peeing. I'm not entirely sure what that was, but it happened.

Then, there were the individuals who did a light whistle. Either one of those short whistles of disbelief because I just went directly to the middle urinal, while others would start whistling an entire tune. I made these moments weird a few times by singing the lyrics and telling the person it was a good song. They just gave a simple "mhm" back to me while they stared into the urinal abyss.

The simple conversation piece in the bathroom was consistent with the first observation. Of course, I was always attempting to start the conversation. Most times, my fellow urinators would struggle to give a response. However, between all the noises and figuring out how to speak while urinating in public next to this weird guy talking to them, they would spit out a straightforward answer of "yeah" or "uh-huh ." I had plenty of moments where people would not respond at all.

An interesting observation of talking at the urinals with these individuals who struggled to respond would be the post-urinal interaction. Some men would strike up a conversation at the sinks based on what I mentioned while we were at the urinals. Sometimes, nothing would be said to me until I was in a study nook or if I had a class with them. I intrigued their brains for whatever reason, and once in a safer situation for them to talk, the conversation would ensue. Sometimes at length. I even made a few friends with these post-urinal observation conversations. Once I explained everything to them, they often laughed and agreed on the unsaid bathroom rules.

There is one group of men that I must give a notable mention to due to the willingness, in many cases, to have a plain old conversation at the urinals and not give two craps about anything. These individuals were older men who had lived life. They had become established in many ways. They had been around a few places and knew a few things. They met plenty of people and had been in a variety of situations. Conversations while urinating in a public bathroom with a stranger? No big deal. I would mention the weather, and they would tell me a snowstorm story. I would say something about sports, and they would dig deep into statistics. These occurrences were only sometimes guaranteed, but they happened more often than not.

One older gentleman enjoyed the conversation so much that he continued talking to me after urinating. He was laughing and joking, not ending the discussion. Then, once he finished peeing, as I was still standing at the urinal, he slapped my back and gave my shoulder a squeeze with his unwashed hands. Thankfully, I fully understood the context of this gesture and gave the benefit of the doubt that it was unintentional at that moment. However, that was crossing a line for even me at the urinals. I still question whether he noticed I was intentional in my actions and was attempting to one-up me in breaking social barriers.

There was one last interesting reaction I noticed during this experiment. The post-urinal facial expressions and/or the lack of eye contact that would occur. On many occasions, I saw people keep their eyes down or away from me in the bathroom after using the urinal. I would take note of individuals immediately after leaving the bathroom, and most would still look away and not make eye contact with me deliberately.

Then there were the people who would make eye contact with me, but you could see one of the two things in their eyes: confusion or anger. You can understand another human's emotions depending on their eyes and how they're looking at you. It was never a stare but a glare long enough to let me know they were confused or upset at me for the situation I just placed them in. I usually would get these looks at the sink or moments after exiting the bathroom. Not always, but sometimes, after an observation, I would see someone from said observation continuing to give me eyes of sustained confusion or anger. I assumed this look stemmed from me using the middle urinal, as I had no other interactions with them.

As these were the more common findings in my observations, I also had a few outliers, which happen in all good research. These individuals took their reactions to the next level.

As pivoting away from me was a typical maneuver, the amount of shifting away depended on the individual. Sometimes, I would only notice a slight pivot; other times, an extreme pivot to where it looked like they were urinating on the wall. However, with one outlier, the pivot became more of a shuffle.

Before I continue I should make clear, if I haven't before, that my intentions were never to be a creep or put anyone into a panic and completely stress them out. I used the middle urinal and created small talk, nothing crazy. I tried to recognize if people were overly stressed and not to push them over their limits. However, I must not have sensed the stress levels well on this day.

As I walked in, another fellow bathroom patron was already at the urinal by the stalls. I started doing my business and then made a statement that was not even a question. I think I said, "Man, what a day," very lightly or something of that nature. I then noticed that this individual's posture shifted to standing entirely straight, with his eyes looking up towards where the wall met the ceiling while taking some deep breaths.

While this occurred, another bathroom participant entered to use the last urinal, and naturally, I asked them how it was going. As this interaction happened, I could hear the pisser beside the stall's breathing rate increase. I did not think anything of it because this new person talked back to me without hesitation, leading to a full-on conversation.

It was a short period that happened quickly, as most of the observations had been. Most men are not at the urinal for a lengthy time. But at some point, the first bathroom patron decided to pinch off his flow and ultimately did a side shuffle, facing the wall the entire time, moving himself into a stall. This maneuver threw me and the other pissing participant off. We just stopped and stared as this happened. Then we shrugged our shoulders, washed our hands, and went on our way, thinking that was an odd moment.

I want to apologize. If that person ever happens to read or hear about this book, I'm sorry.

The next outlier was anger and frustration, leading to minor retaliation.

I did not have much retaliation during this social experiment. The occasional cases where people would tell me, "Please be quiet," or "Why are you talking to me?" or "Seriously, the urinal next to me?" And, of course, some urinators would start muttering things under their breath and not talking to me, as if I couldn't hear them. But one observation that would become my decision to stop observing at the college came from an interaction with an individual who abruptly burst out at me.

My approach to conducting myself in this particular observation was the same. I walked in, and this patron was at the urinal to the left, and the urinal to the right was still open. Without hesitation, I went directly to the middle urinal, as always. While looking down (my zipper was being stupid on this day), I said,

"Man, I can't wait for this semester to be over; I'm ready for summer," as it was close to the end of the semester.

This individual's reaction would then come from the depths of anger I would have never anticipated.

I could sense him staring at me. And when I looked over, he stared directly into my eyes, and I could see rage. I turned my face away and attempted to keep to myself, but the lid was already off. He then, in very colorful language and very loudly, asked if I was hitting on him at the urinals and told me that I was gay. I could hear the anger in his voice as he said this to me.

I responded to him, stating that I did not realize wanting the semester to be over made me gay and that I was making simple conversation. Hindsight, I probably should have just shut my mouth. He then began mumbling things under his breath and shaking his head. I could hear him say something like "this dumb motherf***er" and "this dick-looking b**ch," along with other colorful phrases.

I consciously stood at the urinal for a few seconds longer to allow this person to leave. When he finished at the urinal, he continued to say things under his breath in pure anger about this experience. I heard him at the sink for what seemed like a few minutes as I just stood there at the urinal, and before he exited the bathroom, he made the statement loudly for me to hear, "Don't follow me, you f**king q**er, and we better never cross paths in the bathroom again."

Once he left the bathroom, I remember being there alone for a few minutes, and while washing my hands, I just stared into the mirror. The paper for the class was due soon, and I figured I could do a few more observations out in the community, but at this point, I decided to do no more observations at the college. I thought about this man's reaction and recognized that this was my sign to slow my role.

Little did I know that this interaction with this specific person would not be over. About thirty minutes had passed since the observation, and I wanted coffee. When walking to the little café area at the college, there was a large common area that many students congregated at that I had to walk by. I didn't notice this individual sitting with a group in this area as I passed. I only would recognize he was there as he loudly announced to his group, "There is that dick-looking mother***er from the bathroom I told you about."

And cue the awkward stares towards me and the phrase "dick looker" being randomly whispered by others who heard this being said while this guy pointed at me.

Thankfully, this phrase did not stick in association with me. But I knew for sure this was my sign for me to pump the brakes and no longer be the middle urinal pisser. Beyond this interaction, I knew people had been catching on to what I was doing. Bathroom goers became weary of my presence. With this in mind, along with the time left of the semester, I ended the experiment.

Even though the official experiment time had ended and I needed a break from using the middle urinal, I became more appreciative. When I'm feeling funny and the mood is right, I often use the middle urinal to keep society in check. And it usually never fails to this day; there is some type of reaction from other men by my use of the middle urinal when it's unnecessary and I break the buffer rule.

A Square to Spare:
Insight on Rules of Women's Public Bathrooms

While conducting the middle urinal experiment, I remember thinking about how I was observing specific rules of the men's room, but what about women? Were there rules and methods for the women's bathroom as it is in the men's bathroom?

I figured there might be, just not as distinctive as there is with urinals for apparent reasons. And since it would be highly unethical and illegal for me to sit in the women's bathroom and watch, I needed to have discussions with multiple women to find trends.

I thought of simple questions to create and build a conversation around the women's public bathroom without sounding too creepy (or so I thought). I decided to open with the question, "When you use a public women's bathroom, do you have a method or habit that you use before you choose a stall?" From this, I would ask how they started these habits. I decided on two follow-up questions: "Are there any methods or habits in a public bathroom you do once in the stall?" and "Is there anything you should not do while using a women's public bathroom?"

I used a similar method when conducting group conversations with men on urinal use. It was highly informal. I would find groups with women I had classes with or random groups in a study nook, explain my project, and ask questions. One thing that was very helpful for me by the time I was doing these questions was that some people heard through the grapevine I had been "researching male behavior in public bathrooms," which I would correct them as that seemed too official and told them I was only pissing in the middle urinal. Most women thought it was hilarious, asking what I had observed. They did not know my name but knew I was the middle urinal guy. Having this identified made it easier for them to share tales of the women's public bathroom with me.

The first theme I found in my conversations about the women's bathroom is that it is similar to the urinal buffer rule; instead, it would be considered a stall buffer rule. Many women stated that unless they are with someone they know, they commonly look for feet under the stalls and try to avoid using a stall next to another bathroom patron. When asked why this is, many answered that it's just what they learned, and one participant said, "If there is space, why not give the other person space?"

It was also interesting to note how everyone had a particular pattern when they entered the bathroom while attempting to look for feet. There were two different ways commonly told to me this decision process happens. The first was if the last stall of the row was available, that is the stall of choice, so no one would have to walk past the person going to the bathroom. Some participants expressed concern about others looking in through the doors' cracks while conducting business. However, a few people mentioned that they chose the stall closest to the main door for a quick exit and did not have to do the foot look in a larger, more crowded bathroom. The majority told me this is the decision-making behavior they have acquired from experience throughout life, with no one telling them this was the expectation in public bathrooms.

There was a small amount of conversation participants who openly stated that they immediately choose the middle stalls, but not many. The middle seemed to be the last choice spot for many people's bathroom needs. At least from the conversations I was fortunate to have.

During these conversations, it was recognized how common the hover technique is in women's public bathrooms. Per multiple reports from the conversation participants, it's not uncommon for women to go into a stall (after their process of deciding which stall to use) and find a mess within' its small confines. We're talking a little bit of urine, maybe some tiny splatter of poop, or the occasional blood spotting, and sometimes a used feminine product on the floor or toilet. I'm sure these examples are not happening each time a woman uses a public bathroom, but the point of "would I want to sit on a toilet like that?" was accomplished. I can only assume that some participants shared only the worst public bathrooms they have been in.

Before I explain the hover technique, it's essential to realize that there is no right or wrong, as I am basing my explanation on a variety of descriptions from the commonly mentioned methods provided by only a few conversation participants. The overall grand objective was the same, regardless of the difference in method.

The hover technique involves first a toilet seat cover laid down if possible to not replicate the mess already in existence. Most people clarified that they didn't touch the toilet to complete this step. Instead, they just got close to the toilet and did a little drop over the area with the cover (as the instructions insist on most boxes providing the toilet seat covers in public bathrooms), hoping for the best. Then, clothing garments are maneuvered to around knee height. This next part is where leg strength and balance come into play. Women are not as fortunate as men to have a fleshy piece to handle and aim for quick toileting use as we all know, so they must aim their entire bodies in these instances. With the hover technique, a woman usually has to balance and perform a partial squat to get into the appropriate position to line up with the toilet and complete their bathroom business, hoping for good targeting. The majority then stated they discarded the first few squares of toilet paper in public bathrooms before choosing the squares to use. And everything flushes down the toilet, including the toilet seat cover. No evidence is left behind.

Interestingly, several women, like some of the men, had specific stories about public bathrooms that created their negative mindset if they had one. One story in particular stood out over the others. It involved checking for supplies, such as toilet paper amounts. But it also displayed how human interaction in public bathrooms can become rotten, even during a simple need.

This individual discussed a time at the mall during the holiday season when many claim to be most giving and when the mall is busiest. This individual described having to wait to use the bathroom and having no time to check on how much toilet paper there was, plus every stall was in use except one by the time it was her turn. Once done with the actual task of going to the bathroom, she realized that she had no toilet paper. She had to ask for a square of toilet paper from the other bathroomgoers. This woman stated that asking for a square of toilet paper from strangers is awkward because there is no good approach to this situation.

This individual explained that she knocked on the one-stall wall and said, "Hi, I'm sorry to bother you, but I'm out of toilet paper. Do you have enough to pass some over to me?" She said the person moved their feet away from her stall, saying nothing. Meanwhile, she could hear other women giggling and some mocking her request for toilet paper. Still in need, she knocked on the other stall wall, saying the same thing. This other bathroom patron replied, "What the hell, how do you not have any toilet paper?" The idea of supply and demand during the holiday season did not come to mind, yet she still did not pass a square.

The woman telling me this story continuously emphasized how she needed just one square and was pleading for it. But in those few moments that seemed like forever per the storyteller, she was not getting any toilet paper from anyone else, and she could continue to hear other women mumbling things under their breath as if she was asking for something unethical and disturbing.

Then, when one of the women in a stall next over finished their business, she was heard forcefully pulling toilet paper out as if she were angry. She dropped it on the floor and put her wet, snowy boot on it to push it over, absorbing other fine bathroom juices. The woman remembering this experience said she didn't even pick up the toilet paper because it was sopping wet with snow and other fluids that it would have been pointless…and a cause for an infection.

She accepted defeat since no one would pass her a square politely in a busy public bathroom and just went about her day pissed off because she was pissed on with no square to spare. And yes, this is similar to a *Seinfeld* episode from many years ago, making one wonder when the screenwriters came up with the idea that it must have happened to someone back then. It's interesting to realize that this has possibly been an issue for longer than anyone has spoken of because of the environment in which it takes place.

These discussions discovered that certain rules and patterns are followed when using a women's public bathroom, just as in the men's bathroom. From my understanding of the answers and narratives provided by conversation participants, since a women's public bathroom is not as direct and open as a men's public bathroom due to the setup, the behaved nature is not as recognized. But once thought of the public bathroom process occurred, many women, just like men, have learned and followed specific patterns.

And by the way, looking for feet in stalls is not just a woman thing. Many men do this when they have to take a poop as well.

The Concluding Flush

Once I flushed the middle urinal for the last time while collecting data, I had proven my thesis, gaining significant insight about public bathrooms...probably more than anyone could care to know.

The conversations and observations both created uneasy feelings in their particular ways. Breaking the unsaid rule of the middle urinal buffer disrupted other men from trying to take a quick piss, causing a variety of reactions. At the same time, the conversations displayed that even talking about the bathroom is also inherently taboo.

When I was able to create conversations about public bathroom use, they never ensued without a consistent giggle or laugh from someone. There was always some blushing, stuttering, and eye-rolling from both men and women. It was odd and nerve-wrecking for some to create functional words and statements about going to the bathroom because they had always rightfully kept to themselves until I shook them up, looking for answers. With this, I made conclusions about simply discussing public bathroom habits.

First, it deals with parts of our body identified to keep private in all ways, hence private parts. And for obvious reasons, we are taught that these are private parts because, as we all know, there is more than human waste happening with them. My children and undoubtedly many others understand to hit someone in the groin and stomp on a foot if they are being asked about their privates by someone who shouldn't be asking. Unfortunately, the need to discuss this and enforce these ideas with children has become increasingly critical as issues have become more prevalent. With this mindset, I believe the expectation of keeping our private parts private creates the primary resistance to being able to discuss bathroom habits. It's a red flag if someone doesn't have this resistance.

My second conversation conclusion is that people become disgusted when discussing topics involving urine and feces. And I'm not disagreeing. Our human waste usually has a smell to it while not being pretty to look at. I witnessed some people gag slightly, talking about the scent of their waste. It's usually only discussed in the doctor's office when you notice something might be off in stream, color, amount, or odor. It's not usual to sit in a group and have someone ask everyone about their bathroom routine, hoping to have willing participants.

However, I asked about public bathrooms and just GOING to the bathroom, not about their specific waste and what it looked like. But people naturally associated their human waste characteristics with using the bathroom in any capacity, which makes sense. Thankfully, through motivational conversation, I could work around these barriers and find the motion for the conversation I sought. However, I did learn that people have some weird ways of describing how their urine smells and that many people love how their pee smells after eating asparagus.

As the conversations displayed some hesitancy and unnecessary topics, it also took serious thought by individuals as they had to think about how they operated in public bathrooms. It was mentioned several times by participants that they go into "auto-pilot" when using a public bathroom. There was no thought to what they were doing. Once I posed my questions, some people had to act out their motions of going into a public bathroom to discuss it. Others (usually those who hate public bathrooms with the entirety of their souls) knew where all the less trafficked bathrooms were and could vividly describe their habits with no issue. I assume this is because of the intensity of them not liking public bathrooms and being observant of every inch and second.

The end outcome of the conversations was that there were common beliefs and techniques in public bathrooms. Men and women have similar patterns when using a public bathroom and avoid situations that could be uncomfortable. If someone breaks these barriers, many people admit to pivoting away or moving in closer to the urinal in the men's room or shuffling feet away from the stall next to them in the women's bathroom. One essential action that many reported is that they never make eye contact at any point in a public bathroom and rarely have any conversation. It's strictly business and nothing else the majority of the time.

That leads me to my first conclusion from the observations during the middle urinal experiment. I recognized that communication, eye contact, and socializing are uncommon in a public bathroom. Participants discussed not being social, going back once more to that "auto-pilot" comment when using a public bathroom. I was able to witness this often. I would walk in and attempt to look people right in the eye to say hello and spark some conversation, usually only being given a quick head bob acknowledging my statement or a mumbled hello before they focused back on urinating. I considered myself lucky if I even got that reaction. Trying to create conversation at the urinals was a little much on my part, but there are no rules stating I couldn't try. Of course, I had my small margin of people who would respond to this socially, primarily the older gentlemen with no worries in the world.

Another common area during the experiment where I would attempt to engage in conversation and be a social being was post-urinal use while at the sinks. At this particular moment, people would become more social again, not entirely, but more than at the urinals. During at least half of the observations, when I attempted to converse at the urinals, people would wait to talk back to me until at the sink, either answering my question or beginning to talk about a similar topic. It would throw me off because some people would speak to me minutes after I attempted the initial conversation. But I always welcomed these moments because I would be a creepy asshole if I didn't.

There was an element to these sink-based conversations, though. Most people continued not to make any eye contact. I am unsure of the exact reason, but my strong assumption was that we remained in the bathroom environment. These individuals would stare at their hands while they washed them and talked to me. And no one lingered to continue the conversation. People would always find a way to end the discussion and exit swiftly after washing and drying their hands.

Ultimately, public bathrooms are pure business in everyday life, not for social times. People come to the bathroom with one task in mind, which is eliminating their bodily waste. They want to fulfill this task and be on their way, not have a conversation. It's not like the toilet at home where you could sit for an hour reading or playing on your phone and not truly pooping to get some alone time because, at home, it's just that, being alone and comfortable in your own bathroom. Granted, in public bathrooms, some individuals want to engage in conversation and be social but tend to wait until their genitals are stored back away and are at least conducting the act of washing their hands before jumping onto that social wagon.

The second conclusion is what started this entire experiment, which is the unsaid rule of not using the middle urinal when there is the availability to create the urinal buffer rule. This conclusion stems from both the observations and conversations. Before even doing the observations, men spoke of this unsaid rule without even thinking twice about it. There were no answers to where they learned this behavior, though.

Once I started the observations, I could feel the discontent from the other men at the urinals. I walked up to the middle urinal and conducted my business without any issues or concerns. I recognized that individuals who have to use the middle urinal due to the availability can become hesitant, maybe even a little nerved up, causing them to approach the middle urinal with caution and a lack of confidence that others could notice. Men mentioned during the conversations that even though it's odd when someone is at the middle urinal, they also understand that it's a last resort option in most situations. I was the opposite, using the middle urinal as the only option, and I could tell others sensed it in the bathroom.

Commonly, men will do whatever it takes to place themselves away from another bathroom participant, no matter the condition. The middle urinal experiment displayed this tendency and, at times, the extremes people will take.

As much as I attempted to be social while in public bathrooms, I was not social during each observation. I just used the middle urinal. No matter the circumstances, it was not uncommon to have other men at the urinals pivot away, step in closer to the urinal, or try to finish up quickly and get out. I will admit that there were a few times I did not use the middle urinal, but it was to test this theory. Sure enough, I witnessed no movement when following the urinal buffer rule.

It's also important to note how quickly these actions would occur depending on the situation. If I went to the bathroom and there was only one person at the urinals on my arrival, the pivoting and concealing oneself would happen quickly in comparison to if there was another pissing participant present. The assumption is that this was due to an individual being alone in the bathroom, and there was space for me to spread out. They then felt increasingly threatened because of my actions. But if only the middle urinal was available for use, it was as if the other patrons noted that it was the only open urinal at that time, making it not as urgent to pivot or conduct other movements to shy away. There were times when the pivoting movements or moving closer to the urinal had been so slight I barely recognized them. Of course, when I threw a curveball into the mix and attempted to be social, I would note quicker movement reactions due to making the environment uneasy once again.

As there was not more for me to conclude about urinating in the middle urinal, I realized one conclusion/observation during this that is extremely important for me to discuss. Something I never would have thought about until I was attempting to engage people at the sinks. It's a task that possibly was skipped because people felt nervous about my presence. But sometimes, I didn't even attempt to make the environment awkward other than using the middle urinal, and this action would still not occur. And it has nothing to do with which urinal or stall someone uses in a public bathroom.

This task I speak of is the washing of hands.

Plenty of people would wash their hands with soap and water, while others would rinse them off with water, no soap, which, to me, is still better than not washing your hands at all. But the amount of people I witnessed who did not wash their hands was concerning. On a few occasions, I noticed people wiping their hands off on their pants after using the toilet, but they did not wash their hands, making it questionable what they were wiping off. Let's not mention that I also witnessed a man come out of a stall, in which the smell made it well-known what business he was conducting, and he just walked out of the bathroom, not even thinking about stopping at the sinks.

Here is my public service announcement to anyone reading this.

Wash your hands after using the bathroom and encourage others to do so. Think of it this way. When someone does not wash their hands, they go out into the world touching handles, doorknobs, vending machines, checking out at cash registers, and whatever else, immediately following the bathroom. You end up following behind them, not knowing this fun little fact. Ultimately, you then touch the residue left from their hand that remained after they went to the bathroom and touched their genitals or wiped their butt but failed to wash their hands. And I don't care how much people claim their private parts are clean. They are never spotless and leave a residue on our hands, especially if you get urine dribble and do not wash them.

So wash your hands to stop the spread of infections and bacteria of all kinds, but also so you don't spread the residue from your genitals to everyone else!

Social Awkwardism Beyond The Middle Urinal

The day I created the middle urinal experiment, I was able to highlight the social awkwardness experienced in public bathrooms. I discovered how people learned this behavior through societal actions instead of traditional ways of teaching our children how to act. Beyond the middle urinal, I've continued to have a spark in my soul to be curious about social awkwardism on a larger scale. That curiosity has yet to kill the cat.

I've realized that certain styles and ways people cover their private parts up are acceptable in many parts of the world but not as accepted in America, like men's bikini-cut bathing suits (popularly known as a Speedo). If I were to put on a bikini-cut bathing suit and go to a local beach, people would stare at me as if I were a creeper or have other derogatory ideas. Assumptions would be made about me that would not be factual, instead just based on the fact I would be wearing a male bikini-cut swimsuit. What if I want to tan these pasty thighs? To do so, I would either have to be naked or wear this type of swimwear, and since nudity is not appropriate (nude beaches are the exception), the choice is apparent. But for some reason, many despise the use of these bathing suits for men, even though they cover the genitals.

It's similar to skinny jeans. I've heard people grunt in disapproval about them, and honestly, they're not for me but suitable for those who wear them. The awkward part with them is how skinny they can be and how much people cannot move appropriately in them because of their tightness. It's not uncommon to see people waddling down the road in skinny jeans for style, but functionally, not so much. If we were to observe through the decades, clothing and types of styles have changed with the fads and always will.

Food is a staple to our survival, just like going to the bathroom. Food is socially awkward in our society because of how far away we've become from its natural form. To some people, natural food production is awkward as it has become an unfamiliar trade and art to many. There is a lack of understanding of how our grocery stores become stocked with fresh foods. I have witnessed this over the years as some individuals have been amazed that we own chickens for our eggs. Like it was a hidden secret where eggs came from. Others are occasionally dumbfounded when they look at our garden (which is nothing spectacular), realizing that during the summer months, we can grow a significant amount of food on our own and then freeze extra for the colder months. I also love it when people cringe or cry about the butchering of animals while they eat their fine cuts of steak, chicken tenders, or hot dogs.

Not too far back in our history, it was not uncommon to find many homes throughout the country that owned a few chickens and gardened each year, to only then can, freeze, and store items to help survive throughout the winter months. These were common knowledge skills, but people would also use these techniques for bartering. "I will grow the strawberries and give you some if you grow the corn and give me some" type of deal. Bartering and working together helped create strong communities as they had to rely on one another.

However, not all items were this easy for people to grow and create on their own, like flour and sugar. General stores would sell these items and other needs that were difficult to make or obtain otherwise. But these small stores would last only so long as some intelligent people began mass producing food, causing people not to worry as much about where their food would come from. With the mass production of food, the creation of grocery stores would end up providing the majority of the staples and needs in people's homes. As demand increased, along with the innovation of new types of items to sell, plus taking things further by creating a variety of ready-to-eat meals and taking out the task of cooking altogether, we now have the large and dynamic grocery stores we recognize today. But it has created a disconnect and social awkwardness with our food and the natural order of being able to grow your own or source from a local farmer throughout our communities. And in some belief, it has taken many people away from the art of cooking, lacking understanding of the basic skills to make a dish.

I could deep dive into food topics to discuss and display how people are socially awkward towards food even further. But that is for another day (or just look up some documentaries on Netflix), as it's essential to talk about other everyday staples in our communities that are also considered socially awkward.

Social awkwardism is all around us, whether we accept it or not. Our acceptance and understanding depend upon the community's beliefs we are a part of through facts and opinions provided to us through different outlets. As those facts and opinions become existent through varying messages, it is up to the individual who receives the message to break it down and find their perception from their basis.

News networks often highlight vital socially awkward topics, making people within our communities numb to the discussions and thoughts provided. Politics, race, and sexuality seem to be three primary topics often blasted out into the world from various angles. Many people become guarded and passionately debate with anyone and everyone over these topics, whether they pertain to their everyday lives or not. There is always one person everyone knows who struggles with leaving others' opinions alone and respecting different beliefs without providing their two cents and then some. And cue the social awkwardism.

There once was a time when politicians were not career politicians but rather subject matter experts in an aspect of American life. They ran to be in office to support the American people based on their professional and personal experiences from their communities. They attempted to provide policies and methods to build stronger communities nationwide. These politicians succeeded in our government because the different political parties could sit down and be civil in making decisions together without clouding the process with extreme thoughts or beliefs.

However, civility and understanding ceased to exist a while ago.

In current-day politics, many politicians are still in office for the people, but they tend to have a shadow over them due to the ones who make politics socially awkward with either their extreme beliefs or tactics. Media helps build this social awkwardness by displaying particular agendas and political extremists to viewers depending on which side of the line they are on. These agendas that are put out into our communities by media outlets then help reshape thoughts and ideas for those willing to listen, even if the accuracy of the information provided could be questionable.

Groups in various communities will act out in a manner promoted by those who hold fundamental power because those who hold power did not get there by themselves. It took thoughts and ideas to spread throughout communities willing to listen and be influenced to give that power to an individual. But it goes beyond just the individual. These thoughts, ideas, and influences have often built a fire inside followers throughout the history of many civilizations and governments. Here, in the land of the free, it has created critical tensions among different groups of people. These critical tensions have produced unnecessary disputes between everyday people, who all are just trying to live and survive while enjoying whatever time they have remaining in this world.

A highly debatable but necessary element in all communities that is also talked about in politics and multiple media platforms, along with being essential to the human race and all living organisms since the beginning of time, is sexuality.

Go to an art museum, and you will see sexuality painted hundreds of years ago, with various types of sexual acts or objectification occurring, among other things. It's nothing new or crazy to talk about, but in recent years, we have created a heavy

stigma around the topic of sexuality.

Conversation dealing with sexuality could go in a million

different ways as it has functioned in societies with a high level of

variety, making it difficult to cover it all. Because sexuality is an

instinct that flows through us all in some form or fashion, it allows

for crucial connections to occur and, depending on its appetite, must

be fed regularly.

There is no right or wrong on who one can like and enjoy.

The natural law of attraction takes care of that. If everyone followed

their instincts with sexuality (within' the limits of the law

obviously), there is a strong possibility that positive mental health

stability would occur throughout communities, and people would

feel happier and satisfied, which would then help birth and grow

communities. This idea is only speculation from my brain, of course,

though.

The kicker to sexuality currently is that lines have become

blurred. Many individuals struggle to follow their instincts because of societal beliefs and thoughts. There is uncertainty as to how people respond to sexuality as it has changed and evolved drastically and continues to do so. People shy away from being able to talk about it, while the business markets for sexuality have increased not only in the amount of content but the shock of the content while allowing free range in who provides said content. In today's world, just about anyone can sell feet and hand videos on the internet to others whose law of attraction is into that type of thing.

Our current youth are facing the largest blur within these lines, not just by the explicit content that can be found but also by what ideas and beliefs are going into a variety of aspects throughout entertainment and everyday life. There are no barriers. You can find sex topics, ideas, and beliefs in seven and under programming if you pay attention hard enough to particular undertone messages stitched in. The content is increasingly apparent with sexual messages and ideas in the storyline programming for older children. But how many parents pay attention to their child's show to grasp the content? I bet not many.

I'm not saying there was never some element of sexuality in programming for children in the past or that even this is wrong. But the presentation of ideas has changed drastically. Then, leading into the teenage years, many ideas and beliefs learned through content, among other things, are applied to physical life.

Teenagers are a walking ball of horniness, and as their sexual instincts come into play, they thrive by finding something to feed that instinct. The programming they watched growing up helps with building this mindset and instinct. The internet also provides an immediate substance for this need while creating a poor belief of what sexuality is, not only in private matters with their sexual encounters but in everyday life. Keep your eyes open in various public spaces. Current-day sexuality influence is all over. People often don't see it because, once again, we have become accustomed to these ideas, whether we agree with them or not, ignoring it as we continue on in our lives.

However, the hole of sexuality has been dug deeper for us human species.

We have become too creative, too knowledgeable, and too willing to play against the forces of the biological nature of genetics and natural order. Many decide to make changes in their own right but then push those ideas onto everyone else, even though it was a personal decision.

As humans, we recognize we are one of the most intelligent and technologically advanced species to play against natural forces, but this is also when we should examine all creatures. Simple creatures. The majority of living organisms have two genetic sexes that mate and help build up that organism's presence in their fun ways. For chickens, the rooster dances around a hen, then mounts and practices polygamy. Penguins have a life mate (the male protects and sits on the egg). Male giraffes smell out the female's urine until the time is right. And dogs go into heat.

Unfortunately, there are no specific smells to help us humans turn on sexuality, and in some cases, there is some dancing, but nothing like a rooster. We have complex brains that need more connection to occur intellectually, usually (not always) to help build that thread into sexuality. But it's our complex brains, too, that have created the thought process and techniques of defying natural biology in many ways, from implants to deciding to change gender. These types of choices have increased in popularity while significantly skewing sexuality because one must question if what they're seeing is natural or not. It's gone beyond sexuality and into other concerns throughout our communities, along with professional services due to possible misleading information on official documents. It will be interesting to see if this certain sexuality mindset continues to evolve into something more or if society will decide to recollect their thoughts and begin down a different path.

Politics, sexuality, and plenty of other topics provide everyday social awkwardness throughout our communities, but there is one topic that topples them all. Something your 90-year-old Nana even has been getting into.

Technology advancements have been incredible over the last twenty or so years. It's unbelievable to think about how far it's come. We went from having dictionaries and encyclopedias to Alexa's in our homes and Google at our fingertips. Previously, someone had to take time to find the proper resources when they needed to find answers. Now, people can ask their smart device a question, and BAM! There is the answer. It can help us navigate our entire days, not just in the home but wherever we are, as most have a smart device, also known as a cell phone, on them at all times.

Cell phones are the most significant advancement as they have become an essential tool in many people's lives. People no longer put their home phone number down as a contact because their cell phone is usually always with them, allowing access to them no matter where or when. Plus, many people no longer have a phone line established in their homes due to cell phones, making long corded phone conversations a thing of the past.

Businesses and organizations have advanced and changed with the times as well. Many, if not all, have created applications and other means to use their services right at your fingertips, no longer needing to get on a computer or physically enter an establishment. Social media and other forms of entertainment have also taken advantage of creating applications at our fingertips. With this access and advancement, many people throughout our communities would struggle without its daily use.

Even though cell phones and their resources are great tools, they have created the ultimate social awkwardness. It has assisted in people losing touch with normal conversation on the phone and in person. Texting has become a top means of communication, and many people do not even use actual words or sentences. Instead, they abbreviate entire messages or use emojis. With face-to-face conversations, individuals have increasingly struggled over the last decade to maintain a conversation with another person. Establishing proper eye contact while watching the other person's facial expressions, listening to what is said, allowing it to register in the brain, and then providing a proper response.

That's how humans are supposed to communicate with one another.

The biggest culprit in creating this type of dysfunction is social media. People cannot hold a conversation, or they start sweating while in a crowded room, but will post something new every day on their "socials." Post videos of themselves on different servers for hundreds or thousands, if not millions, of people to see, depending on the provided content and allowed audience. They then absorb the comments and "likes," which make them feel good. They provide comments and "like" other social media user's posts and pictures. These online interactions are the new normal, replacing much of basic daily physical conversation to provide us with similar feelings. But when that screen turns off, many people are alone. So it's easy to just turn the screen back on to go back to feeling the good vibes from social media.

I have witnessed many things when it comes to cell phone use. One of the most striking times was once in a restaurant a few years ago. The number of people sitting at tables with their cell phones out amazed me. They were not creating conversation at the table but were looking down at their screen doing whatever. Then, they took pictures of their food but also took pictures with others at the table with them as if they all conversed and had a great time, yet they were looking at their phones the majority of the time. From then on, I kept a mental note of this habit in restaurants, among other areas, noticing this trend in various public places. Next time you go out to eat, take a moment and look around you. I hope I'm wrong and you don't witness this.

And please understand that I do not disown cell phones and technology. I'm with the societal rules and have my cell phone, using it often for all the necessary things and unnecessary stuff. In the morning, I drink coffee and scroll through social media to see what craziness I can find. I check out what my friends worldwide are up to because it is an amazing tool for keeping connected. I also hang out with Alexa occasionally, having a dance party to various music as I randomly think of songs and blurt them out to blast on the speakers.

The kicker is that I'm self-aware. I can set it down when I've had too much and walk away. Go outside and enjoy nature. I know how to be present with others around me, giving them my attention and making that connection that is strived for in physical conversation. And many people understand these concepts as well, being able to have limits, create boundaries, and set their technology down. It's a matter of just making it normal for everyone to follow.

However, the younger crowd, who have been submerged in technology as it has become continuously familiar in everyday life while surviving through factors like shutting down for a pandemic and increasing technology use, are in a particular dilemma, which is a lack of skills for proper communication without technology. Even bullying (which is not okay in any form) has shifted from in-person to cyberbullying. Looking at the bigger picture, this may eventually create a complex and unique dysfunction in our society (if it has not done so already), with the only solution being to revert to a life without all the technology. But again, this is all just a matter of opinion.

Overall, all great civilizations had and have a level of social awkwardness because all things are weird until they become normalized. However, some things are still awkward once normalized; instead, we learn to ignore it and let it happen as a society. But as a society, we do not always consider how it affects those within the community and what outcomes will come from it, affecting generations to come years from now. History books display that change occurs eventually for all great civilizations, usually by the younger generations experiencing the repercussions of the older generations as they acknowledge the issues at hand and create solutions. But if we just stopped and took our time to self-reflect on the world we live in now and how we could make it the most sustainable, we could leave it flourishing for generations to come.

If you asked me about a solution, I would tell everyone to take a breather and let's talk about history. It's easy not to look back at our history to understand how communities found ways to establish themselves while certain lifestyles became hammered into existence. But history is a double-edged sword that tells us how we arrived at our current day while providing the plans and ideas for continued building. We can be angry and upset with certain parts of history but leave it as a lesson learned, not the means for revenge. History is the blueprint to find solutions and create stronger, unified communities.

Of all things to try and make sustainable, I think urinating in the middle urinal might always be unacceptable. I do not see that rule changing any time soon. But I will keep at it and encourage all other men to do so!

If You Shake It More Than Three Times, You're Playing With It

Bathrooms are everywhere. Restaurants, grocery stores, schools, dollar generals, gas stations, and if you're a thrill seeker, you can find port-a-potties in all kinds of weird places. We need them to dispose of our human waste safely for a variety of reasons, but also so our world doesn't have a urine-drenched, turd scent around us. Going to the bathroom for most people is a multiple times a day, everyday deal. So it's not like it's a choice to do it because our bodies will naturally make sure going to the bathroom occurs to maintain homeostasis. It depends on the individual where they decide to conduct this business, hoping they're potty trained and don't go in their pants or on the floor.

But as the entirety of this book has displayed, speaking about our bathroom habits or breaking common unsaid rules of public bathrooms is either odd or inappropriate. No matter how often we visit a porcelain bowl throughout our days, unless an issue, it is rarely discussed. And when you do, people become red, embarrassed, and at a loss for words, sometimes struggling to make complete sentences.

But the middle urinal experiment is something more in thought than just discussing the use of public bathrooms.

I decided to share this social experiment story, hoping that others will slow down and see the world surrounding them, recognizing the natural and unnatural order and how we as a society can be the only ones to change it. Our world is rapidly accelerating at the current time, making it easy to forget how to slow down and take a few moments to acknowledge everything around us and where we are.

Change takes work to happen. And it's not always clear what the change should be. There are many ideas on what changes should occur, but usually, the true answer is not immediately in the forefront. It takes time, failure, and persistence to find that answer. However, it also takes communities to be understanding and willing to work with one another. And to work with one another, people must make connections and relationships appropriately, which also takes time. As communities come together, they must have open ears to ideas beyond their beliefs and the confidence to expand further than they ever imagined. Otherwise, they will remain in a hole, only to go deeper. Change helps create the ladder out.

Small steps are what will bring that confidence and change. With that, ask yourself what small changes you can make to enhance and strengthen yourself and your community. Put the cell phone down and have a conversation, even if it's with a stranger. Smile at random people to make it infectious. Recognize the issues and the good in the streets around your home. Understand reality and what is not, making sure our young know the difference, too. Create conversations with our youth and others that could become awkward, but it is a fact of our life that they must understand how it works and what they might encounter. The ultimate goal should be to interact with others and create a sense of community in various fashions with no tools or assistance, just human-to-human.

And if there is one first small step, it's as simple as this. Use the middle urinal. Pass the person in the stall next to you toilet paper.

Have a conversation while washing your hands. Create a community in these small, awkward moments to build more significant moments later, even in a public bathroom.

www.ingramcontent.com/pod-product-compliance
Lightning Source LLC
Chambersburg PA
CBHW070954250726
48663CB00002B/212